We're MOVING to the MOON!

BLOOMSBURY

To Andrew, who said I should write a book
about humans returning to the Moon.
Love you to infinity and beyond x – C.C.

To Anna – H.W.

BLOOMSBURY CHILDREN'S BOOKS
Bloomsbury Publishing Plc
50 Bedford Square, London, WC1B 3DP, UK
Bloomsbury Publishing Ireland Limited
29 Earlsfort Terrace, Dublin 2, D02 AY28, Ireland

First published in Great Britain 2026 by Bloomsbury Publishing Plc

A catalogue record for this book is available from the British Library

ISBN: HB: 978-1-5266-7720-4
PB: 978-1-5266-7721-1
eBook: 978-1-5266-7719-8

2 4 6 8 10 9 7 5 3 1

Printed and bound in China by Leo Paper Products, Heshan, Guangdong

MIX
Paper | Supporting responsible forestry
FSC® C020056

To find out more about our authors and books visit www.bloomsbury.com and sign up for our newsletters
For product safety related questions contact productsafety@bloomsbury.com

Written by
Catherine Cawthorne

Illustrated by
Harry Woodgate

We're MOVING to the MOON!

Blast off on a fact-filled space adventure!

BLOOMSBURY
CHILDREN'S BOOKS
LONDON OXFORD NEW YORK NEW DELHI SYDNEY

Our family doesn't do normal holidays. My mum and dad and big brother Tom are all about **ADVENTURE**.

We've swum the Amazon on river dolphins.

We've climbed the Himalayas on huge woolly yaks. Backwards.

We've ballet-danced at the bottom of the Mariana Trench.

But Mum and Dad have really gone and done it this time. For our next ADVENTURE ...

we're going to LIVE on the MOON.

I'm not quite sure HOW we're going to live on the Moon.

It's just a big, grey, dusty rock, isn't it?

Mum says we should start getting ready. She's just given me this packing list …

Tom says he only planned to pack one pair of pants anyway, but that's because he's

STINKY.

We can't take much with us because we have to keep our spaceship as light as we can, so I'm only packing **ABSOLUTE ESSENTIALS**.

Scruff Scruff and Sir Pine Cone are absolute essentials, though! Has anyone taken a toy into space before?

You're going to have such a brilliant adventure! And you're coming back to see us at Christmas, remember?
Grandpa and Grandma
Stinky Tom
Love, Kit xxx
HELLO! From the Himalayas
But the Moon is such a long way away, and you won't be able to come for tea on Wednesdays.
We can still talk to you on Wednesdays! Even the very first astronauts on the Moon could make a phone call. They used a radio to talk to people on Earth. And guess who they talked to?
Their grandma and grandpa?
No, the president of the United States of America!

The very first people to ever walk on the Moon were two astronauts called Neil Armstrong and Buzz Aldrin. They landed on 20 July 1969 – more than 50 years ago!

They did some science experiments, collected lunar rocks and soil, took photos and planted a USA flag.

The U.S. President rang and talked to them using a radio.

It was the longest-distance phone call anyone had ever made!

After the first 12 astronauts, humans didn't walk on the Moon again for more than 50 years!

5... 4... 3... 2... 1... BLAST OFF!

NASA's SLS (Space Launch System) rocket weighs almost 3 MILLION KILOGRAMS – about the same as 8 jumbo jets. It goes so fast it could travel full circle around the Earth in just over an hour!

Taking off was so scary! It was so

NOISY

and

SHAKY ...

... and it felt like I had a

herd of elephants

standing on my chest, pushing me into my seat!

But now – WOW – we're in actual space ... this is incredible! It's calm and quiet here (apart from Tom's singing. SO ANNOYING).
LA, LA, LA, LA!
Look! We've detached from the main part of the rocket, because we don't need it anymore. We're flying the rest of the way in just the top part.
Are we almost there, Helix?
Earth
Mercury
Venus
Mars
Jupiter
Saturn
Neptune
Uranus
The Moon
Not even close! The Moon is about 384,400 kilometres away from Earth. You could fit all the planets in the Solar System between the Earth and the Moon and still have some space left over. It will take us just over three days to get there.
What? More than three WHOLE DAYS! And I'm strapped in next to Tom!
HEEEEEEEEEEEEEEEEEELP!
2.5 days later ...
I spy with my little eye something beginning with 'S'.
Not stars AGAIN?
Yes.

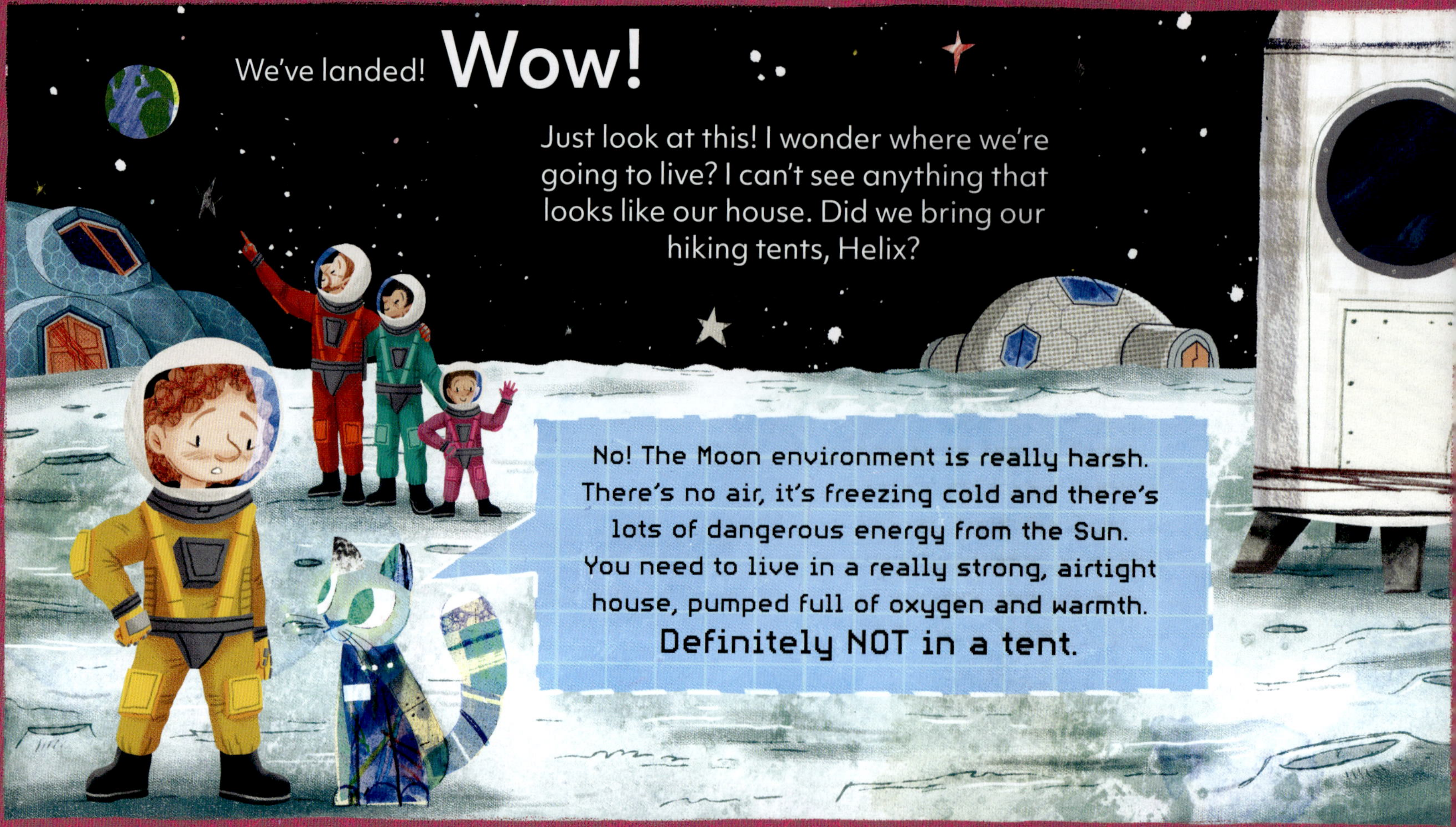
We've landed! Wow!
Just look at this! I wonder where we're going to live? I can't see anything that looks like our house. Did we bring our hiking tents, Helix?
No! The Moon environment is really harsh. There's no air, it's freezing cold and there's lots of dangerous energy from the Sun. You need to live in a really strong, airtight house, pumped full of oxygen and warmth.
Definitely NOT in a tent.

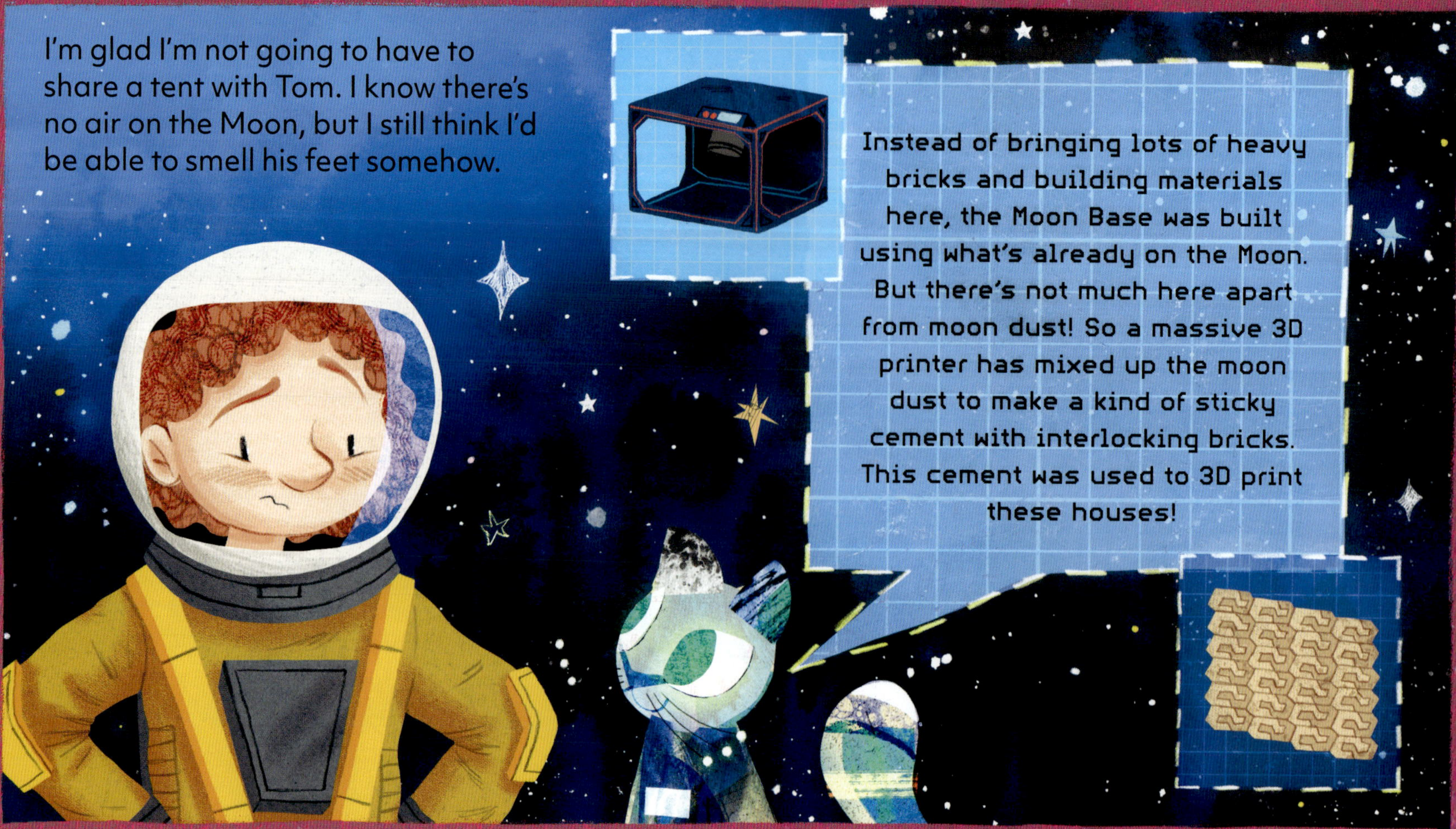
I'm glad I'm not going to have to share a tent with Tom. I know there's no air on the Moon, but I still think I'd be able to smell his feet somehow.
Instead of bringing lots of heavy bricks and building materials here, the Moon Base was built using what's already on the Moon. But there's not much here apart from moon dust! So a massive 3D printer has mixed up the moon dust to make a kind of sticky cement with interlocking bricks. This cement was used to 3D print these houses!

Ta-dah! Here we are, everyone. Our new space home!

This doesn't look like a normal house! I'm not sure about this. I hope it has a loo, because I really need a wee!

Scientists have discovered a huge, deep cave on the Moon that was formed millions of years ago by hot lava. One day, a cave like this might be used as a Moon Base, because living underground protects astronauts from the cold, meteors and solar energy waves. Just so long as there aren't any undiscovered giant space badgers living inside them already ...

Where's the loo, Helix?
I need to go ...
RIGHT NOW.
I hope it's not like going on the spaceship, because that was complicated ...
There is *some* gravity here to stop all your poos and wees floating off around the house, which we can all be pleased about. Not like the spaceship!
OK, OK – show me!
Welcome to NASA's Universal Waste Management System! It's a cross between a toilet and a hoover. There isn't enough gravity here for everything to drop neatly from your bottom into the toilet, so you need some suction! It also recycles your wee into water. It's important not to waste anything in space.
A few moments later ...
That was kind of fun! I can't wait to tell Grandma and Grandpa about the Wee Hoover!

Whilst you're learning about the toilet, do you remember that I'd put nappies on the packing list?
Yeah ...
Mum says when I'm outside on the Moon, I have to wear a spacesuit. If I suddenly need a wee, I can't just go behind a bush – partly because there are no bushes, but mainly because there's no oxygen. So I have to wear a Maximum Absorbency Garment, which is a fancy way of saying 'a nappy'.
Just in case.
I'm not sure Tom was listening though.

My tummy's beginning to
RUMBLE!
I wonder what's for dinner?
Tom's probably not that hungry because he eats his
OWN SNOT.
What was the first thing anybody ever ate in space, Helix?
MMM... BEEFY
The first person to travel into space was called Yuri Gagarin and he ate BEEF AND LIVER PASTE from a toothpaste tube! At least he then got to eat a pudding of chocolate spread, also from a tube. Nobody was sure whether the human body would even be able to swallow in space, but he was fine.

Mum says it's teatime, but this does **NOT** look like pasta and tomato sauce! We've got **INSECTS** and **SALAD** for tea! I suppose that's better than beef and liver paste from a toothpaste tube …

NASA's Deep Space Food Challenge asked lots of companies globally to invent ways of growing healthy, tasty food in space. Scientists in Thailand found a way of mixing insects and other ingredients to create special 'bio inks' for 3D food printers to make good food!

Another company is making BioPods (fancy greenhouses) that can grow fruit and vegetables in space.

Today, Dad's going to teach me how to be a space farmer! We have to grow our own fruit and vegetables here because the supermarket doesn't deliver to the Moon! But it can't be that hard, can it?

What do plants need to grow?

But it's tricky to grow things on the Moon. There's no air, it doesn't rain, the temperature can go from freezing cold at night to boiling hot in the day, and there's only Moon dust on the ground instead of soil. Oh, and night-time lasts for two weeks here, too.

Gardening on the Moon: Choosing which fruits and vegetables to grow …

- The plants need to be good for your body, to keep you healthy
- They should not take up too much space when they grow
- They should have a strong flavour as astronauts find that food doesn't taste as strong in space

Plants also need food to help them grow. You could use your own wee. It is 95 per cent water, and also contains chemicals that help plants to grow. People on Earth have been using wee for gardening for years and years. And we know how important recycling is in space!

10:28AM Tues 18 Oct

From: kit@lunanet.com
To: grahamandedith@livingonearth.net
Re: Football on the Moon!

Dear Grandma and Grandpa,

Guess what? I played football on the Moon! It was SO cool! We had to use a special big football filled with something called aerogel, because a normal football would burst here. I could kick the ball sooooooooo far, it was like superhero football. Mum says footballs travel six times further here than on Earth because there's no wind or air resistance and a lot less gravity.

We had to be really careful not to bump into each other because we all had our oxygen tanks and spacesuits on. This meant Tom couldn't cheat and do dodgy tackles, ha ha! He also couldn't complain to the referee because the referee was a hologram!

The pitch is made of moon dust which has been melted with a laser, so that the dust doesn't all fly up in a big cloud around us. The pitch is covered by a big net so we can't lose the ball. In moon football you're allowed to bounce the ball off the netting. Dad says it's a bit like a mixture of squash and football, so he keeps calling it squootball. (Nobody else does!)

I miss you lots and lots.
I hope you're having fun on Earth.
I wave to you every night!

Lots of love,
Kit xxxxxxx

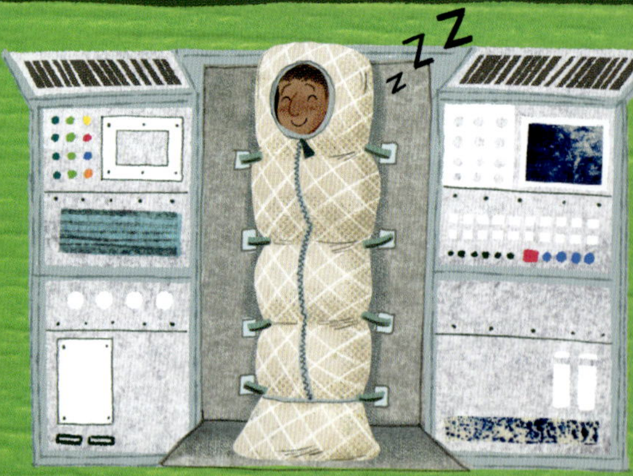

Astronauts on the International Space Station have to strap themselves into bed, because without gravity, they'd just float off! The Moon does have some gravity, so you don't need straps, but you will feel very light on the bed.

The blackout blinds are up, and Dad has put a weighted blanket on me. I've got my cosy pyjamas on, and I've got Scruff Scruff. But I'm never going to sleep.
I'm on the ACTUAL MOON!
Who were the first ever people to sleep here, Helix?
It was Neil Armstrong and Buzz Aldrin. But it did not go well for them as there was no Moon Base back then. They had to sleep in their big bulky spacesuits, and they didn't have any beds! It was noisy, bright, cold and cramped. And because they were so excited, they didn't really sleep at all!
I'm sooooo tired now! Maybe instead of counting sheep, I'll count alien spaceships capturing Tom.
1... 2... 3... zzzzzzzzzz......

Earth is like an enormous magnet. There is an invisible shield around it called a magnetic field which protects it. Compasses work by pointing to Earth's magnetic North Pole. But the Moon has a very weak magnetic field, so Tom's compass won't work. The planet Jupiter has a strong magnetic field, so don't forget to pack your compass if you ever go on holiday there, Kit!

We're driving around the rims of some of the Moon's craters, which are big round holes in the ground. These ones are called 'craters of eternal darkness' because they never get any sunlight. It sounds like a good place for space vampires to live ...

Some craters haven't seen sunlight in billions of years and are EXTREMELY cold as the Sun's rays never reach into them.

Mum is using a SatNav system to navigate so we won't get lost!

This mountain looks

ENORMOUS!

Hey, let's go up there and call Grandma and Grandpa on the radio! Tom, can you give me a piggyback? Pleeeeease?

For SatNav to work on Earth, your phone or tablet needs to be able to receive signals from at least three satellites that are orbiting the Earth. It uses those signals to work out where you are. Astronauts on a Moon Base will also have a SatNav system, because there will be a system of satellites orbiting the Moon that do the same job.

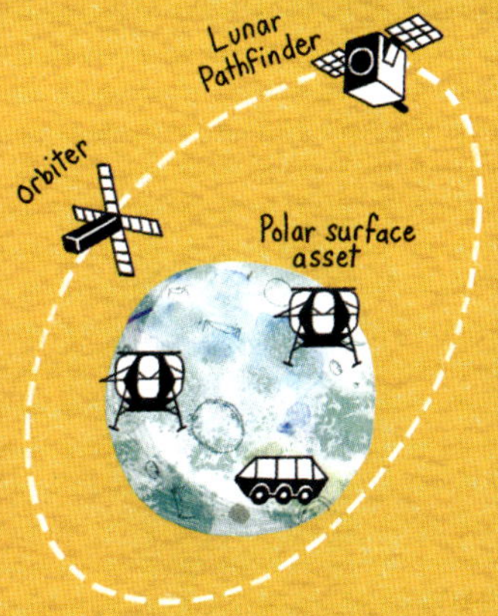

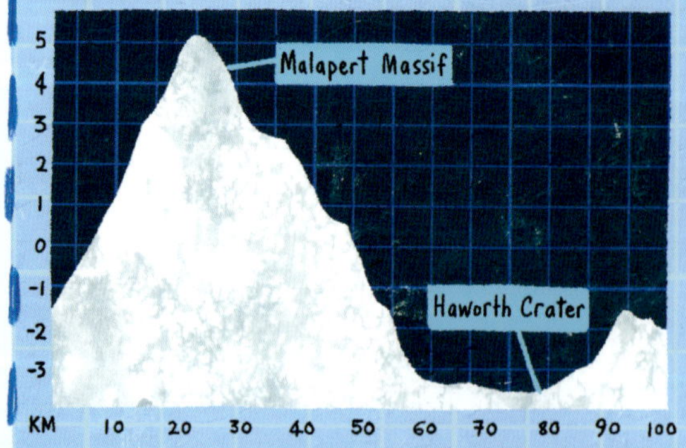

Malapert Massif, near the Moon's South Pole, is over 5,000 metres tall. But it's next to Haworth Crater, so if you measure from the bottom of the crater to the top of the mountain, it is about the height of Mount Everest!

Hello? ... Hello? ...
Can anybody hear me?
Grandma?
Grandpa?
Helix, it isn't working!
Using a radio won't work on this part of the Moon. The signals are going the wrong way. Sorry Kit, I have to shut down now ...
But I don't know how to get back without you!
We're lost!

Mum? Dad? Where's Kit?
We thought she was with you.
No! She's upset because I wouldn't take her up the mountain.
This is all my fault!
Let's try not to panic. I'll switch bright lights on the Moon buggy so she can see where we are.

She can't have gone far.
Use the Lunar Search and
Rescue system to find her.

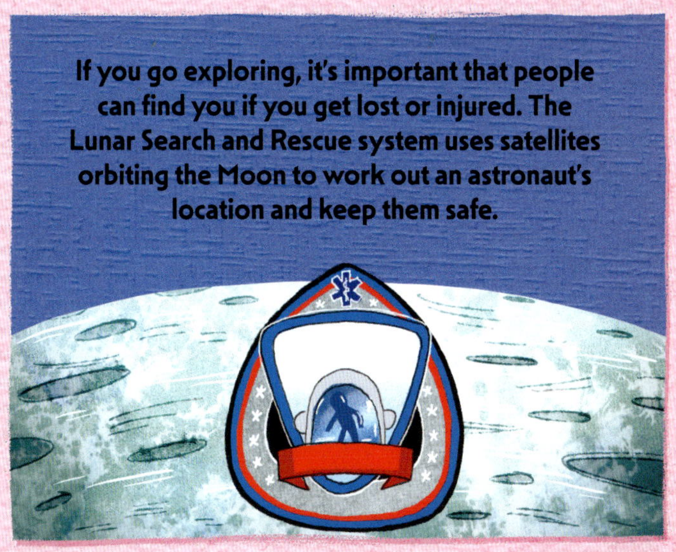
If you go exploring, it's important that people can find you if you get lost or injured. The Lunar Search and Rescue system uses satellites orbiting the Moon to work out an astronaut's location and keep them safe.

Helix? Helix?
Don't leave me.
I'm almost there, she's
really close now ...

KIT!
How did you find me?
Easy, I just followed the smell of your STINKY socks.
You can't even SMELL on the Moon!

I'm SO happy to see you, Mum and Dad!
It was scary being lost. You were right, Helix. It's not safe!
I am always right, Kit. I am a robot.

Before we go back to the Moon Base, Dad says we can listen for aliens! Technically, we're all extraterrestrial beings because we're a family living on the Moon! I already knew Tom was an alien. Helix, are there any other creatures on the Moon?
Maybe! In 2019, a lander crashed here with some tardigrades or 'water bears' on board. They are tiny creatures that can survive virtually anything. It is possible that some of them are still on the Moon, although scientists think they probably didn't survive the crash landing.
Awww, a water bear!
Cute!
I wonder if Mum and Dad would let me keep one?
They are too small for humans to see, so they would not make very good pets, Kit.

The best places to look for aliens are on planets in The Goldilocks Zone – planets that are not too hot, not too cold but just the right temperature for water. Just how Goldilocks likes her porridge! All living things that we know of need water, so planets that might have water are a good place to start looking. So far, scientists have found 16 planets in Goldilocks Zones. (As far as we know, none of these contain porridge or bears.)

The far side of the Moon is a great place to use radio telescopes and to listen to the very furthest, deepest places in the universe. It faces away from Earth, so it isn't affected by all the signals and noises that humans make. So if any aliens say, 'WE ARE COMING TO DESTROY YOU!' or 'STOP NICKING MY DONUTS, NEIL!', it will be loud and clear.

The longer I stay, the more I think I'll like it here.
Nobody back on Earth will believe I've been exploring on the Moon and listening for aliens.
Can I ring Grandma and Grandpa? It's great here but I do miss them.
Yes, don't forget, Dad says we just have to wait for the satellites to be in the right position, remember?
The Moon's satellites communicate with the Moon Base when they're flying over the South Pole and then communicate with Earth when they're on the near side.

Tom's going to tell me when it's time.
I'm just going to do something whilst we're waiting ...
That's awesome Kit. Time to ring Grandma and Grandpa now!
Tom
Love, Kit xxx
Greetings, Earthlings!

Six months later ...
I thought we were going back to Earth to see Grandma and Grandpa for Christmas. But guess what? They've come to see us instead! This is the best Christmas ever!
It's been so fun showing them around. They loved the greenhouse, and the research lab and our house ...
... but their favourite thing to do is jumping around in their spacesuits!
Wheeeeeeeee!
I feel so young!

It's time to open our presents.

Remember Sir Pine Cone? I brought him with me and planted him! Dad and I have been watering him secretly in the greenhouse. I've checked in on him every day. Now look at him!

HAPPY CHRISTMAS!

KIT AND TOM'S GUIDE TO THE MOON!

Name: The Moon

Age: 4.5 billion years old

Just think of all the birthday candles – Kit

Size: About a quarter of the size of the Earth. If the Earth was the size of a basketball, the Moon would be the size of a tennis ball. The surface of the Moon is about the same size as the continent of Africa.

A bit like Grandpa – Tom

Appearance: Grey and dusty. Covered in pits called craters, which are caused by meteorites, comets and asteroids crashing into it.

Temperature: 127°C in full sunlight to –173°C in the bottom of craters in the darkness.

Even colder than ice cream – Kit

Distance from Earth: It changes! The shortest distance is 360,000 kilometres away and the furthest is 405,000 kilometres. But it is also moving about 4 centimetres further away from Earth every year.

DID YOU KNOW?

When the Moon first formed, it was waaaaaay closer to Earth than it is now, and an Earth day was only six hours long!

'The gravitational pull of the Moon is what creates the tides of the sea on Earth'.

When astronauts make footprints in the dust on the Moon they could last for about 10 million years because there's no wind.

When Krakatoa erupted in 1883, it sent tiny particles into the air that blocked red light and let blue light through. This made the Moon look blue for almost two years.

By following patterns of moonlight, dung beetles use the Moon to navigate in a straight line.

The Moon doesn't make its own light. When we see it shining in the sky, we are seeing sunlight bouncing off its surface.

There are more than 890 moons orbiting planets and asteroids in our Solar System. Earth's Moon is the fifth largest.

The dark patches you can see when you look at the Moon (called lunar maria) used to be seas of molten lava.

Glossary

astronaut A person whose job is to travel and work in space.

gravity A pulling force. Here on Earth, gravity pulls things to the centre of the Earth, which is why things fall to the ground when we drop them. There is gravity on the Moon, but it is not as strong because the Moon is smaller than the Earth. The Sun's gravity keeps all the planets in orbit around it.

International Space Station (ISS) A large spacecraft orbiting Earth, where astronauts live and do scientific research.

lunar Anything associated with the Moon. For example, a lunar buggy is a vehicle that has been made to travel on the Moon.

NASA The space agency of the United States of America. It stands for 'National Aeronautics and Space Administration'.

orbit A regular, repeating path that one object in space takes around another object. You are in orbit right now because the Earth orbits the Sun!

Malapert Massif A mountain on the Moon near the Moon's South Pole.

Moon Base Human-made buildings on the surface of the Moon. Humans haven't built a Moon Base yet, but there are plans to do it in the future. This book is set in the future, when a Moon Base has already been built.

satellite Something that orbits something else in space. The Moon is a natural satellite because it orbits the Earth. Artificial satellites are machines sent into space to travel round the Earth, the Moon or another planet to collect information or for communication.

Solar System Our Sun and all of the things that orbit (or travel round) it. This includes the eight planets and their moons, dwarf planets, asteroids and comets.

Numbers

Some of the numbers mentioned in this book are very big and hard to imagine.
Here they are in order:

One hundred	**100**
One thousand	**1,000**
One million	**1,000,000**
One billion	**1,000,000,000**

One last thing ...

Did you notice that Kit and Tom's dad has a prosthetic (artificial) leg? The twelve astronauts who walked on the Moon during the original Moon landings were all white, American, able-bodied men. But space should be for everyone. An astronaut called John McFall, who has a prosthetic leg, has been working with the European Space Agency to see whether he could go into space. Their tests have found that he absolutely **can**!